To Gary Ann, my sister,
courageously facing down lung cancer
—*N. G.*

I am steeped in humble appreciation and gratitude to the men
and women, both seen and unseen, involved in the civil rights movement.
We are all indebted to Mrs. Rosa Parks and her dear friend Johnnie Carr,
as well as Dr. Martin Luther King, Jr., and many others,
for their amazing strength and push for change.
—*B. C.*

AUTHOR'S NOTE

Rosa Parks is: a cooling breeze on a sweltering day; a sun-dried quilt in fall; the enchantment of snowflakes extending the horizon; the promise of renewal at spring. It is an honor and a responsibility to explore the bravery of her acceptance of history's challenge.

ILLUSTRATOR'S NOTE

In researching this story, I made a trip in August 2004 to Montgomery and Selma. When I arrived in Alabama, the first thing I noticed was the heat. That is why my paintings for this book have a yellow, sometimes dark, hue. I wanted the reader to feel in that heat a foreshadowing, an uneasy quiet before the storm. Even though the story of Rosa Parks and the bus boycott began in Montgomery, Alabama, in 1955, it did not end there. Many future marchers—in Selma and elsewhere throughout the country over the next decade—were inspired by the courage of Mrs. Rosa Parks. In my paintings, Mrs. Parks looks as if light is emanating from her. To me, she is like a radiant chandelier, an elegant light that illuminates all our many pathways.

Henry Holt and Company, LLC, *Publishers since 1866*
175 Fifth Avenue, New York, New York 10010 [www.henryholtchildrensbooks.com]

Henry Holt® is a registered trademark of Henry Holt and Company, LLC.
Text copyright © 2005 by Nikki Giovanni. Illustrations copyright © 2005 by Bryan Collier.
All rights reserved. Distributed in Canada by H. B. Fenn and Company Ltd.

Library of Congress Cataloging-in-Publication Data
Giovanni, Nikki. Rosa / written by Nikki Giovanni; illustrated by Bryan Collier.—1st ed.   p.   cm.
ISBN-13: 978-0-8050-7106-1 / ISBN-10: 0-8050-7106-7
1. Parks, Rosa, 1913– —Juvenile literature. 2. African American women—Alabama—Montgomery—Biography—Juvenile literature. 3. African Americans—Alabama—Montgomery—Biography—Juvenile literature. 4. Civil rights workers—Alabama—Montgomery—Biography—Juvenile literature. 5. African Americans—Civil rights—Alabama—Montgomery—History—20th century—Juvenile literature. 6. Segregation in transportation—Alabama—Montgomery—History—20th century—Juvenile literature. 7. Montgomery (Ala.)—Race relations—Juvenile literature. 8. Montgomery (Ala.)—Biography—Juvenile literature. I. Collier, Bryan, ill. II. Title.
F334.M753P38427 2005   323'.092—dc22   2005002160

First Edition—2005 / Designed by Patrick Collins. The artist used watercolor and collage to create the illustrations for this book. Printed in Mexico.

3   5   7   9   10   8   6   4

Rosa

Nikki Giovanni

illustrated by **Bryan Collier**

Henry Holt and Company ✦ New York

Mrs. Parks was having a good day. Mother was getting over that touch of flu and was up this morning for breakfast at the table. Her husband, Raymond Parks, one of the best barbers in the county, had been asked to take on extra work at the air force base. And the first day of December was always special because you could just feel Christmas in the air.

Everybody knew the alterations department would soon be very, very busy. Mrs. Parks would laugh each year with the other seamstresses and say that "those elves in the North Pole have nothing on us!"

The women of Montgomery, both young and older, would come in with their fancy holiday dresses that needed adjustments or their Sunday suits and blouses that needed just a touch—a flower or some velvet trimming or something to make the ladies look festive.

Rosa Parks was the best seamstress. The needle and thread flew through her hands like the gold spinning from Rumpelstiltskin's loom. The other seamstresses would tease Rosa Parks and say she used magic. Rosa would laugh. "Not magic. Just concentration," she would say. Some days she would skip lunch to be finished on time.

This Thursday they had gotten a bit ahead of their schedule. "Why don't you go on home, Rosa," said the supervisor. "I know your mother is feeling poorly, and you might want to look in on her."

The supervisor knew Rosa would stay until the work was done, but it was only December 1. No need to push. Rosa appreciated that. Now she could get home early, and since Raymond would be working late, maybe she would surprise him with a meat loaf, his favorite.

"See you in the morning." Rosa waved good-bye and headed for the bus stop. She fiddled in her pocket for the dime so that she would not have to ask for change. When she stepped up to drop her fare in, she was smiling in anticipation of the nice dinner she would make. As was the evil custom, she then got off the bus and went to the back door to enter the bus from the rear.

Rosa saw that the section reserved for blacks was full, but she noticed the neutral section, the part of the bus where blacks or whites could sit, had free seats.

The left side of the aisle had two seats and on the right side a man was sitting next to the window. Rosa decided to sit next to him. She did not remember his name, but she knew his face. His son, Jimmy, came frequently to the NAACP Youth Council affairs. They exchanged pleasantries as the bus pulled away from the curb.

Rosa settled her sewing bag and her purse near her knees, trying not to crowd Jimmy's father. Men take up more space, she was thinking as she tried to squish her packages closer. The bus made several more stops, and the two seats opposite her were filled by blacks. She sat on her side of the aisle daydreaming about her good day and planning her special meal for her husband.

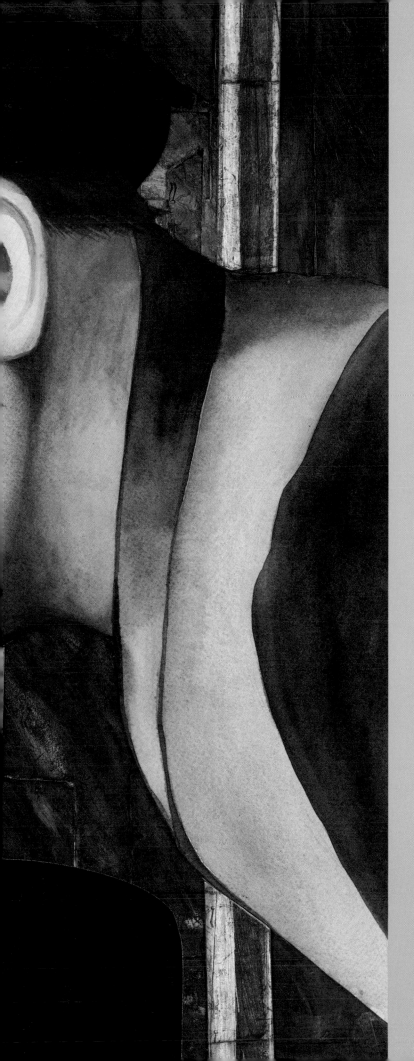

"I said give me those seats!" the bus driver bellowed. Mrs. Parks looked up in surprise. The two men on the opposite side of the aisle were rising to move into the crowded black section. Jimmy's father muttered, more to himself than anyone else, "I don't feel like trouble today. I'm gonna move."

Mrs. Parks stood to let him out, looked at James Blake, the bus driver, and then sat back down.

"You better make it easy on yourself!" Blake yelled.

"Why do you pick on us?" Mrs. Parks asked with that quiet strength of hers.

"I'm going to call the police!" Blake threatened.

"Do what you must," Mrs. Parks quietly replied. She was not frightened. She was not going to give in to that which was wrong.

Some of the white people were saying aloud, "She ought to be arrested," and "Take her off this bus." Some of the black people, recognizing the potential for ugliness, got off the bus. Others stayed on, saying among themselves, "That is the neutral section. She has a right to be there."

Mrs. Parks sat.

As Mrs. Parks sat waiting for the police to come, she thought of all the brave men and women, boys and girls who stood tall for civil rights. She recited in her mind the 1954 Brown versus Board of Education decision, in which the United States Supreme Court ruled that separate is "inherently unequal."

She sighed as she realized she was tired. Not tired from work but tired of putting white people first. Tired of stepping off sidewalks to let white people pass, tired of eating at separate lunch counters and learning at separate schools.

She was tired of "Colored" entrances, "Colored" balconies, "Colored" drinking fountains, and "Colored" taxis. She was tired of getting somewhere first and being waited on last. Tired of "separate," and definitely tired of "not equal."

She thought about her mother and her grandmother and knew they would want her to be strong. She had not sought this moment, but she was ready for it.

When the policeman bent down to ask "Auntie, are you going to move?" all the strength of all the people through all those many years joined in her. Rosa Parks said no.

Jo Ann Robinson was at the Piggly Wiggly when she learned of the arrest. She had stopped in to purchase a box of macaroni and cheese. She always served macaroni and cheese when she baked red snapper for dinner. A sister member of the Women's Political Council approached her just as she reached the checkout lane.

"Not Mrs. Parks!" Mrs. Robinson exclaimed. She then looked furtively around. "Pass the word that everybody should meet me at my office at ten o'clock tonight," she said.

Mrs. Robinson was also Dr. Robinson, a professor at Alabama State, the college designated for "Colored" people, and she was the newly elected president of the Women's Political Council. She rushed home to put dinner on the table, cleaned up the kitchen, and put the kids to bed. She kissed her husband good-bye and hurried to the college. It was dark when they finally gathered.

The twenty-five women first held hands in prayer in hopes that they were doing the right thing. After all, they were going to use the stencil maker, printer, and paper of Alabama State without permission. If they were caught at the college, they all could be arrested for trespassing. But they were working to undermine a vicious law. They decided they would stand under the umbrella of courage Rosa Parks had offered, keeping off the rains of fear and self disgust.

The women quickly formed groups to carry out each task. Making the stencils was the most difficult because the machine keys had to be struck very hard so that the letters would be clearly readable. If a mistake was made, the whole page had to be thrown out; it took a lot of concentration.

The posters read: NO RIDERS TODAY; SUPPORT MRS. PARKS—STAY OFF THE BUSES; WALK ON MONDAY. The women made enough posters for almost every citizen of color in Montgomery. The next morning, as people read the posters, they remembered the joy they felt when the Supreme Court declared that separate was not equal. They were sure that once the highest court in the land had spoken, they would not be treated so badly. But that was not the case.

Soon after the ruling, Emmett Till, a fourteen-year-old boy in Money, Mississippi, was viciously lynched. At his funeral, more than one hundred thousand people mourned with his mother. She left his casket open, saying, "I want the world to see what they did to my boy." Now, only weeks after his killers were freed, Rosa Parks had taken a courageous stand. The people were ready to stand with her.

They came together in a great mass meeting: the Women's Political Council, the NAACP, and all the churches. They needed someone to speak for them, to give voice to the injustice. Everyone agreed that the Reverend Martin Luther King, Jr., would be ideal. "We will stay off the buses," Dr. King intoned. "We will walk until justice runs down like water and righteousness like a mighty stream."

People from all over the United States sent shoes and coats and money so that the citizens of Montgomery could walk. Everyone was proud of their nonviolent movement. And the soul force that bound the community together would sustain many marchers for the years of struggle that were yet to come.

And the people walked. They walked in the rain. They walked in the hot sun. They walked early in the morning. They walked late at night. They walked at Christmas, and they walked at Easter. They walked on the Fourth of July; they walked on Labor Day. They walked on Thanksgiving, and then it was almost Christmas again.

They still walked.

Open here ➤

EDMUND PETTUS B

← Open here

On November 13, 1956, almost a year after the arrest of Rosa Parks, the Supreme Court of the United States ruled that segregation on the buses, like segregation at schools, was illegal. Segregation was *wrong*.

Rosa Parks said no so that the Supreme Court could remind the nation that the Constitution of the United States makes no provision for second-class citizenship. We are all equal under the law and are all entitled to its protection.

*The integrity, the dignity,
the quiet strength of Rosa Parks
turned her no into a* YES *for change.*